I know you are probably thinking "I barely make enough to make ends meet how can I possibly have enough to save?" Don't worry I got you!!! If you got our last book, then you learned to round-up on your bills which means you have money have left over. No amount in this book is over $5 and the goal is to save a minimum of $500. Some months you may fail and others you may succeed, but the goal is to never give up. If you finish one month early and still have extra then flip to the back and start one of the "extra credit" pages.

You saved $38 this month!!!

Martin Luther King Jr.

I HAVE A DREAM

You saved $45 this month!!!

You saved $33 this month!!!

You saved $53 this month!!!

You saved $28 this month!!!

You saved $34 this month!!!

You saved $48 this month!!!

Merry Christmas

You saved $44 this month!!!

Lets do some extra credit saving!!!

You saved $57!!!

TIME TO SQUARE UP!!

You saved $50!!!

WALL ART

You saved $50!!!

PIECE OF THE PUZZLE

You saved $50!!!

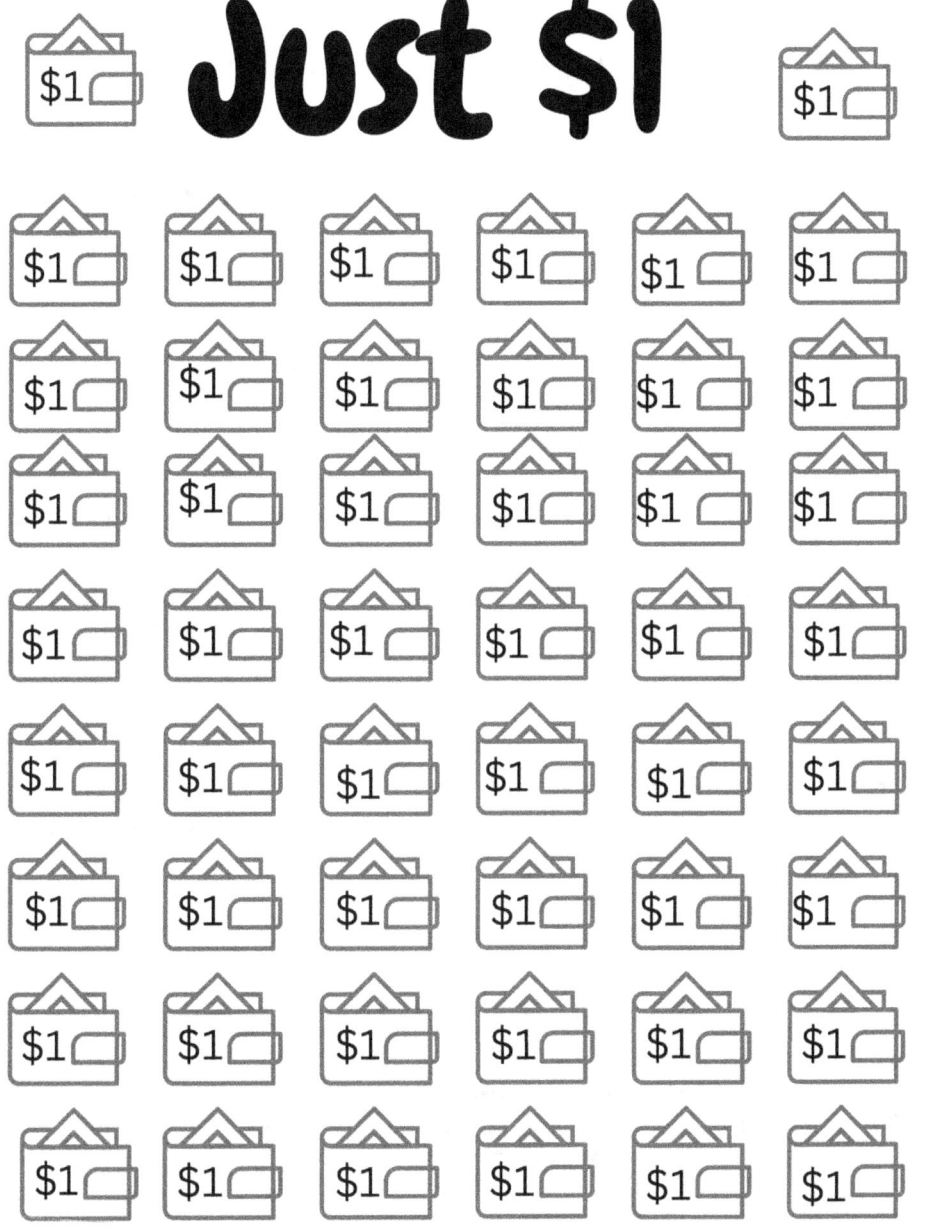

$1	$1	$1
$1	$5	$1
$1	$1	$1

Square

$1	$1	$1
$1	$5	$1
$1	$1	$1

Up

$1	$1	$1
$1	$5	$1
$1	$1	$1

You saved $39 !!!

NOTES

Monthly Savings	= $474
Extra Credit	= $356
Grand Total	= $830

Not to bad for someone who didn't believe they could save $500!!!

www.ingramcontent.com/pod-product-compliance
Lightning Source LLC
Chambersburg PA
CBHW071223240526
45470CB00018B/2298